SNAP SCIENCE
GET YOUR TEETH INTO IT!

PUPIL
WORKBOOK
YEAR 5

Contents

Forces and mechanisms

Properties and uses of materials

Earth and space

Plant and animal life cycles

Separating mixtures and changing materials

Human growth and reproduction

Module 1

Forces and mechanisms

Lesson 1 — What is the friction between different surfaces?

Key vocabulary

force   force meter   friction   Newton (N)   precise

Activity 1: True or false?

This activity revisits learning on forces. Read each statement and tick (✓) if it is true or false.

	True	False
Forces only make objects slow down.		
Forces can change the speed of an object.		
Forces can change the shape of an object.		
Magnetism is a contact force.		
A push is an example of a non-contact force.		
Forces cannot be seen so cannot be measured.		

Activity 2: Reading force meters

There are different sizes of force meter. You need to choose the correct force meter for the force being measured.

Write the measurement shown on each force meter. (Remember to write the units).

Put a tick (✓) above the force meter that would be best to measure a force of 15 N.

Put a star (*) above the force meter that would be best to measure a force of 0.8 N.

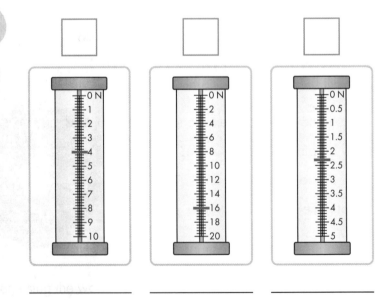

Activity 3: What is the friction between different surfaces?

Set up an enquiry to measure the force required to drag a matchbox over different surfaces.

Draw and label a diagram to show how you are going to measure the friction caused by the different materials.

Which surface do you predict will create the lowest friction? _____

Which surface do you predict will create the highest friction? _____

Record your results in this table.

What I am changing:	What I have observed/measured (in units):

Activity 4: Conclusion

Complete the sentences.

The _____ caused the greatest friction. The _____ caused the least friction.

As the texture of the surface became _____ , the force of friction produced _____ .

This is because _____

_____

Activity 5: What is friction?

Use the learning in this lesson to write a definition for friction below. Use the words below to help you.

friction	force	object	surface	slow

Friction is _____

_____

Key learning

In this lesson I have learnt that: A **force** is a push or a pull. **Friction** is a force that makes it harder to move an object across a surface. If an object is moving, friction slows it down. The force of friction can be measured using a **force meter**. Force is measured in **Newtons (N)**. It is important to choose the correct meter to be able to take **precise** measurements.

Homework

Look for examples of where friction happens, at home or outside. Choose one example. Draw a picture of an example and explain the impact of the friction produced.

Key vocabulary

| air resistance | contact force | dependent variable |
| gravity | independent variable | non-contact force |

Activity 1: Falling objects

Drop a scrumpled ball of paper and a flat sheet of paper from the same height and observe what happens.

Which piece of paper fell to the floor the fastest?

_____

Can you explain why? Use the term 'air resistance' in your answer.

_____

_____

_____

_____

You will need:
- a scrumpled ball of paper
- a flat sheet of paper

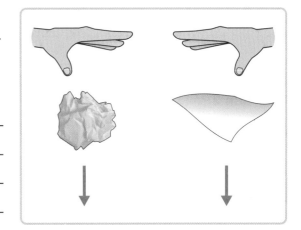

Activity 2: Identifying variables

In an investigation, the independent variable is the variable you change. The dependent variable is the variable you measure.

Imagine you are investigating the effect of the size of a parachute canopy on how quickly it falls.

Sort the following statements into possible independent variables and dependent variables and add them to the table on the next page.

canopy

distance moved sideways	area of parachute canopy
material of parachute canopy	time taken to reach the floor
weight of body	loudness of sound on landing

Independent variable	Dependent variable

Add one extra example of an independent variable and one extra example of a dependent variable to the table.

Use the variables you have identified to design some scientific questions you could investigate.

Question 1

_____

_____

Question 2

_____

_____

Question 3

_____

_____

Key learning

In this lesson I have learnt that: **Gravity** is a **non-contact force** that pulls all objects towards the centre of the Earth. **Air resistance** is a **contact force** that slows down objects as they move through air. Air resistance acts in the opposite direction to the way an object is moving. So if an object is falling, air resistance acts upwards. In an investigation, the **independent variable** is the variable you change. The **dependent variable** is the variable you measure.

Homework

With adult supervision, make your own small parachute at home. Can you design it to fall as slowly as possible when you drop it?

Key vocabulary

air resistance   contact force   gravity   non-contact force

Activity 1: How does the size of the canopy affect the time it takes a parachute to fall?

Investigate the enquiry question 'How does the size of the canopy affect the time it takes a parachute to fall?' by changing the size of the canopy.

Write down your prediction with reasons.

_____

_____

_____

Circle the line graph that best fits your prediction.

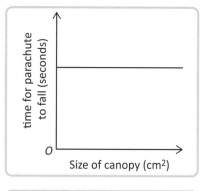 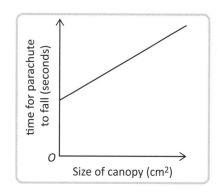 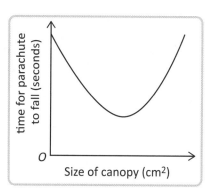

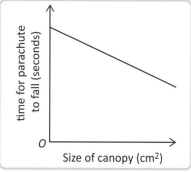 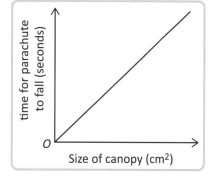 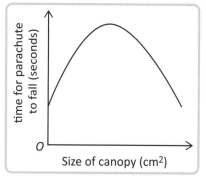

Explain why you chose that graph.

_____

_____

Activity 2: Results

Create four parachutes with different sized canopies, but the same size weights. Measure the size of the canopy of each. Drop each parachute from the same height five times and work out the average time of the fall.

Record your measurements in the table below.

Parachute	Area (in cm²)	Time to fall (in seconds)					
		Try 1	Try 2	Try 3	Try 4	Try 5	Average
1							
2							
3							
4							

Activity 3: Looking at your results

Draw a graph of your results.

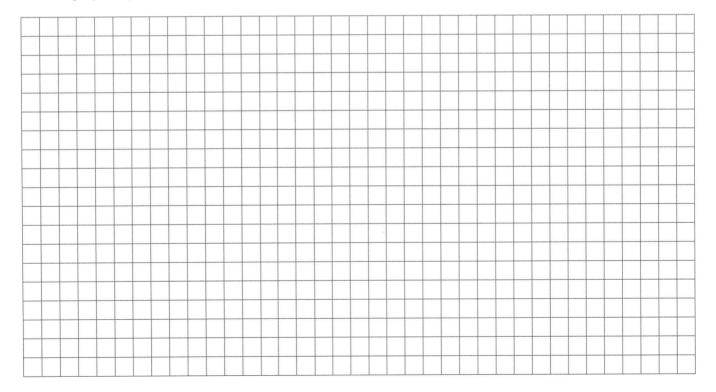

Does the graph look the same as the one you predicted? Explain how it is the same or different.

_____

_____

_____

Activity 4: Conclusion and evaluation

When writing an evaluation you should talk about precision and accuracy:

- Precision depends on the equipment and method used.
- Accuracy is how close to the true answer measurements are. It is improved by taking repeat readings and keeping variables the same.

Complete the sentences below:

I expected the time for the parachute to land to _____ as the size of the parachute

_____ because _____

_____

The results support/refute this because _____

_____

We increased the precision of our measurements by _____

_____

We increased the accuracy of our measurements by _____

_____

I could improve my results by _____

_____

Key learning

In this lesson I have learnt that: **Air resistance** is a **contact force** that slows down objects as they move through the air. **Gravity** is a **non-contact force** that pulls all objects towards the centre of the Earth. The amount of air resistance, and therefore how much an object is slowed down, depends on the surface area of the object.

Homework

Skydivers jump out of aeroplanes. They use parachutes to help them to fall safely down to Earth. Find out about another way that parachutes are used to slow things down.

Key vocabulary

force   oppose   water resistance

Activity 1: How does the shape of an object affect its movement in water?

You will need:
- 3 balls of modelling clay
- a measuring cylinder
- a jug of water
- a stopwatch

Investigate how the shape of an object affects how it moves in water.

Model your clay into three different shapes.

Draw the three shapes of modelling clay you will be testing.

Shape 1	Shape 2	Shape 3

Predict which shape will fall the fastest and why.

_____

_____

Activity 2: Results

Fill the measuring cylinder with water. Drop each shape into the water in turn. Time how long it takes for each shape to reach the bottom of the cylinder. Try each shape five times and work out the average.

Record your measurements in the table on the next page.

Shape	Time to fall (in seconds)					
	Try 1	Try 2	Try 3	Try 4	Try 5	Average

Activity 3: Conclusion and evaluation

Complete the sentences below:

I expected Shape _____ to fall through the water fastest because _____

_____

The data supports/refutes this because _____

_____

We increased the precision of our measurements by _____

_____

We increased the accuracy of our measurements by _____

_____

I could improve my data by _____

_____

Key learning

In this lesson I have learnt that: **Water resistance** is a **force** that slows down an object moving through water, or on the surface of water. It **opposes** the movement – this means it acts in the opposite direction to the way the object is moving. The amount of water resistance depends on the shape of the object.

Homework

Using what you have learnt today, design a boat which has the lowest amount of water resistance possible. Bring in your model or picture next lesson. You could even try it out!

Lesson 5

How does the number of pulleys affect the force needed to lift a load?

Key vocabulary

force   load   mechanism   pulley

Activity 1: How do pulleys work?

Label the diagram to show how a pulley works.

Use the terms:

rope	load
pulling force	pulley

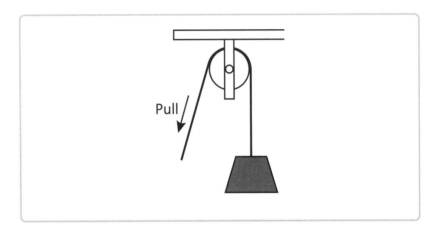

Pull

Activity 2: How does the number of pulleys affect the force needed to lift a load?

Create four different pulley systems with 1, 2, 3 and 4 pulleys (cotton reels) to lift a 1 kg weight. Use a force meter to measure the force required to lift the load with different numbers of pulleys (cotton reels).

Record your results in the table.

You will need:

- 1kg weight
- a ball of string
- a piece of dowelling
- 4 cotton reels
- force meter

Number of pulleys	Force to lift the load (Newtons)					
	Try 1	Try 2	Try 3	Try 4	Try 5	Try 6

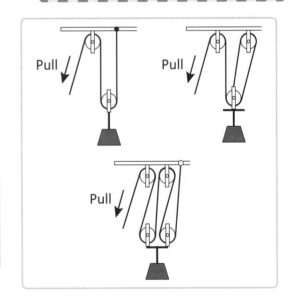

Pull   Pull

Pull

Activity 3: Plotting your results

Plot your results as a bar chart using the average reading. Give your graph a title.

Title: _____

Activity 4: Conclusion

Complete the sentences below.

The data shows that as the number of pulleys increases _____

_____

Using this pattern, I predict that using five, six and seven pulleys, the forces required will be

_____ and _____ and _____ .

Key learning

In this lesson, I have learnt that: A **mechanism** is a device that makes it easier to move something. One type of mechanism is a **pulley**. This is used for lifting **loads** (heavy objects). A pulley lifts the load by applying a pulling **force** at one end of rope that passes over a wheel. The other end of the rope is attached to the load.

Homework

Look for examples of pulleys in your home or outside. Take photographs or draw pictures to share with the class.

Key vocabulary

force   fulcrum   lever   load   mechanism   pivot

Activity 1: How does the length of the lever affect the force needed to lift a load?

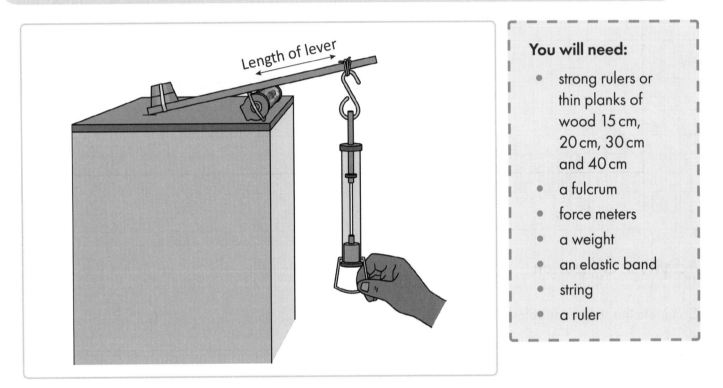

Length of lever

You will need:

- strong rulers or thin planks of wood 15 cm, 20 cm, 30 cm and 40 cm
- a fulcrum
- force meters
- a weight
- an elastic band
- string
- a ruler

Place a lever on a fulcrum and a weight on one end of the lever. Use a force meter to measure the force required to lift a load with different length levers.

Record your results in the table. Complete the headings.

Length of the lever (in _____)	Force to lift the load (in Newtons)					
	Try 1	Try 2	Try 3	Try 4	Try 5	Average
5						
10						
15						
20						

Activity 2: Plotting your results

Plot your results as a line graph using the average reading. Give your graph a title.

Title: _____

Activity 3: Conclusion

Complete the sentences below.

The data shows that as the length of the lever increases _____

_____

Using this pattern, I predict that using a 25 cm lever the forces required will be _____ N

Key learning

In this lesson I have learnt that: A **mechanism** is a device that makes it easier to move something. One type of mechanism is a **lever**. A lever is a long, rigid arm that rests on a pivot. A force is applied to the lever to lift the load at another point on the lever.

Homework

Look for examples of levers in your home or outside. Choose one and draw a diagram of how it works.

Key vocabulary

force   gears   mechanism

Activity 1: Constructing gear systems

You will need:
- gears of different sizes
- cork boards

Use at least three different-sized gears, with different numbers of teeth, to make four different gear systems.

Draw each of the gear systems you made. Add labels showing which way the gears moved.

Activity 2: Looking at gears

In the picture below, gear A rotates clockwise. Which way will gears B, C and D move? Write 'clockwise' or 'anticlockwise'.

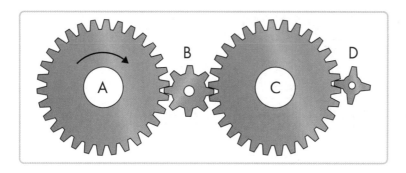

B _____ C _____ D _____

Which gears will turn at the same speed? _____

Which gear will turn the fastest? _____

Activity 3: How do gears work?

Complete the sentences below using the words in the box to help you.

| rotate |
| clockwise |
| anticlockwise |
| teeth |
| faster |
| slower |
| force |

If a gear is rotating clockwise, the gear next to it will _____

The smaller the gear _____
_____

The larger the gear _____
_____

Key learning

A **gear** is a **mechanism** that reduces the **force** required to make something move, making it easier to move. Gears can also change the direction that something moves. Gears are wheels that have teeth that slot together with the teeth on another gear. When one gear is turned, it turns the gear next to it. This gear rotates in the opposite direction.

Homework

Have a look at, or find out about, the gears on the back wheel of a bike. Which size gear wheel makes it easier to pedal? Which size gear wheel would you use if you are travelling quickly?

Properties and uses of materials

Lesson 1 How can we compare and group materials?

Key vocabulary

criteria/criterion   gas   liquid   material   observe   property   solid

Activity 1: Comparing materials

Look at the two objects below. What materials are they made from? What properties could describe them? Draw lines to link the objects to the words you think describe them.

| rigid | transparent | opaque | flexible | magnetic |

| permeable | elastic | durable | absorbent |

Find two more objects. Describe them to a partner, using the words above.

Activity 2: Classifying properties

Choose different materials and observe their properties. Use the grid
to classify them as a **solid**, **liquid** or **gas**. Then add your own sorting
criteria, such as flexible, rigid, transparent, magnetic, to the table.
Write the objects in the table then tick (✓) the properties each has.
One has been done for you.

	Solid	Liquid	Gas	Rigid		
metal key	✓			✓		

Compare your completed grid with your partner's grid. Do your materials share any properties? Are there
any differences?

_____

_____

_____

_____

Use your findings to write about how we can compare and group materials.

_____

_____

_____

_____

Activity 3: Comparing solid objects

Choose two solid objects. Use this grid to compare your objects. Add one more question at the end of the grid.

You will need:

- Two different objects, for example a block of butter, a brick

Object 1:	Comparison	Object 2:
	How easy is it to change the solid's shape?	
	How hard is it?	
	What is its surface like?	
	What would happen if it was heated?	
	What would happen if it was cooled?	
	What would happen if you tried to cut it?	

Key learning

In this lesson I have learnt that: Objects are made from different **materials**, for example metal, wood or plastic. We can **observe** the **properties** of a material. For example, a material could be soft, flexible, and transparent. Most materials have more than one property. We can use different **criteria** to compare and group materials.

Homework

Look out for new buildings being built in the locality. Make a note about how the buildings are being made and what materials are being used. If there are no new buildings nearby, look at existing buildings or buildings on TV.

Key vocabulary

durable   fragile   property   wear and tear   weathering

Activity 1: What do building surveyors do?

Read the information below and complete the activity.

I am a building surveyor and I am here to tell you about my job. Building surveyors like me check the quality of the construction of buildings, from houses to huge skyscrapers. We check the condition of the buildings and suggest ways they can be improved. We use lots of science in our work, so I think of myself as a scientist.

When I inspect a building, I carry out safety checks to make sure it is safe. I check the structure and the inside of the building to ensure the materials and the different parts of the building all meet the safety requirements.

I also carry out quality control checks to ensure a building is fit for human habitation – that means that the living or working environment is acceptable. I also complete an energy check on buildings: I check that that the building is energy efficient.

I work with other scientists such as architects, builders, carpenters, electricians and engineers.

Look at these images of building materials. Choose one that would pass building checks and one that would not pass. Complete the sentences below to explain.

timber with woodworm   rusted steel   crumbling brick   steel   double glazing   roof tiles

The _____ would pass a building surveyor's checks because

_____

_____

The _____ would not pass a building surveyor's checks because

_____

Activity 2: Surveying your school

You are a building surveyor. Check your school building for signs of wear and tear or weathering. Think about:

- what properties make the materials fit for purpose
- whether the materials are at risk of wear and tear or weathering
- whether a different material could be used.

Use this table to record details of five materials that you see. Collect as much information as possible.

Material, use and location					
Properties that make it fit for purpose					
Are there signs of wear and tear or weathering?					
Is it still fit for purpose?					
Should it be repaired or replaced?					

Activity 3: Writing a report

Look at your survey results. Identify the five worst cases of wear and tear or weathering. Note down here what the damage is, why it has happened and what should be done about it. You could present your findings to your head teacher so they can see what improvements need to be made.

Area of our school: _____

_____

Area of our school: _____

_____

Area of our school: _____

_____

Area of our school: _____

_____

Area of our school: _____

_____

Key learning

In this lesson I have learnt that: Many different materials are used to construct a building. Each material must have the right **properties** for its purpose. For example, steel is used for strength and **durability**. Slate is **fragile** but waterproof, so it is good for roof tiles. All materials can be affected by **wear and tear** and **weathering**, so materials must be chosen carefully at the start of a building project.

Homework

Design a home that would be really well insulated and made from environmentally friendly materials and renewable resources. How would you stop heat escaping from your home? What features would you include? What would the building surveyor say when he or she visited to inspect your home?

Key vocabulary

comparative test   liquid   property   solid   viscosity/viscous

Activity 1: Solid or liquid?

Look at the images of sugar and milk being poured. Are they both a liquid? Explain why or why not.

sugar

milk

_____

_____

Activity 2: Comparative test enquiry: viscosity of liquids

You are going to carry out a **comparative** test to investigate the viscosity of different liquids. Work with a group to decide on a method to test how fast each liquid flows.

What liquids are you going to test?

_____   _____

_____   _____

_____   _____

What method will you use?

_____

_____

What equipment will you need?

_____

_____

What evidence will you collect? Think about what you can measure and how you will record it.

_____

_____

Draw and label a diagram to show how you will carry out your investigation.

Carry out your investigation. Draw a table and record your results.

Activity 3: Results

Draw a bar chart to display your results. Annotate your bar chart to order the liquids from thinnest to thickest.

The title of my chart is _____

This chart is to record _____

Which liquid has the lowest viscosity? _____

What kind of scientific enquiry have you carried out? _____

Key learning

In this lesson I have learnt that: **Liquids** flow, or can be poured. A **property** of liquid is its **viscosity**. This describes how fast it can flow. Liquids like yoghurt have a high viscosity and flow slowly. Liquids like water have a low viscosity and flow quickly. Some **solids** can behave like liquids, but they are still a solid.

Homework

Research a recipe for eco-friendly slime that you can make with an adult at home. Can you make your slime more viscous and/or less viscous?

Key vocabulary

flexible   property

Activity 1: Thinking creatively

Look at the image on the right. Answer the questions about it below.

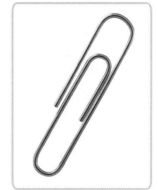

What is this for? _____

What is it made from? _____

What properties does it have? _____

Here are some creative uses for a paper clip.

Smart phone mount

Emergency hem repair

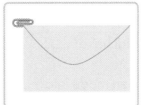

Letter opener

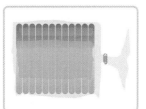

Emergency bread tie

Money clip

Hang ornaments

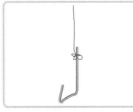

DIY fish hook

Emergency key chain

Can you think of another use for a paper clip? Draw your idea in the space below.

Activity 2: Design your own invention

Choose one of these three items: a paper cup, a wooden chopstick or a piece of waterproof fabric, then answer the questions below.

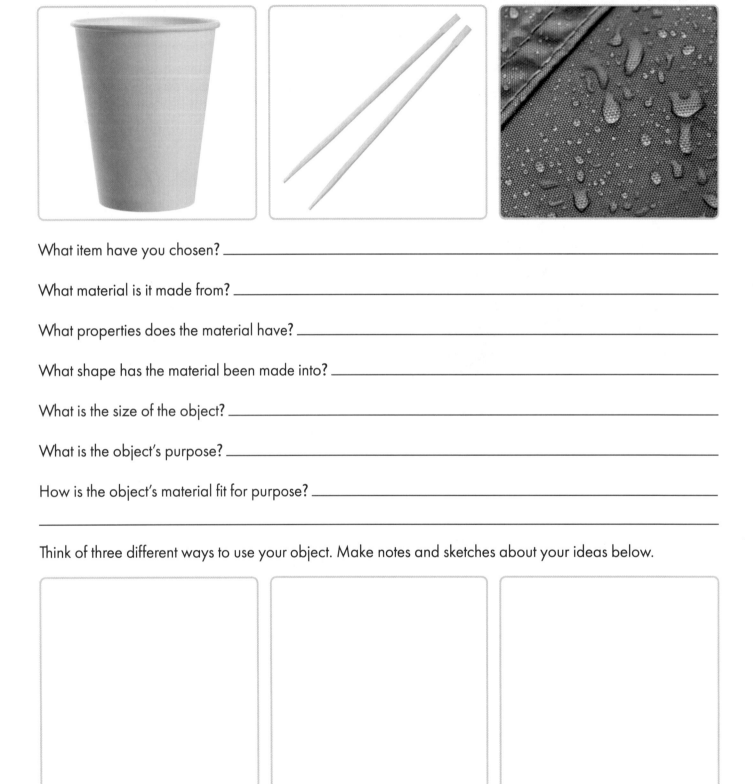

What item have you chosen? _____

What material is it made from? _____

What properties does the material have? _____

What shape has the material been made into? _____

What is the size of the object? _____

What is the object's purpose? _____

How is the object's material fit for purpose? _____
_____

Think of three different ways to use your object. Make notes and sketches about your ideas below.

Activity 3: My final design

Choose one of your three ideas to develop into your final invention. Use this table to explain what it is and how it works. Think about how you would promote your invention and try to come up with a slogan that would make people want to use it.

Details	Annotated drawing
Name of design:	
Purpose:	
Materials:	
Properties of the material:	
Slogan:	

Key learning

In this lesson I have learnt: Inventors use science and design to create and test new things. They choose materials with the right **properties** that will help their invention to work properly. They test their inventions over and over again to see if any improvements are needed.

Homework

Find an object at home. Could it be used another way? Think about its properties and how they will make it suitable for its new use.

Key vocabulary

thermal conductor   thermal insulator

Activity 1: Cool bags

Imagine you are planning a picnic. You will need to take both hot and cold foods, like jacket potatoes and ice lollies. You have two identical cool bags made from the same material. Will they keep the potatoes hot and the ice lollies cool? Tick (✓) the statements about cool bags below that you agree with.

It's called a cool bag for a reason. ☐

It's designed to keep things cold, not to keep things hot! ☐

I think the potato will cool down in the bag. ☐

I think the potato will stay hot. ☐

I think the ice lolly will melt. ☐

I think the ice lolly will stay frozen. ☐

The cool bag is a thermal insulator. ☐

The bag will stop the temperature of whatever is inside from changing. ☐

It will work for hot things and cold things. ☐

I think something else! ☐

Activity 2: Comparative test enquiry: how do cool bags affect hot and cold food?

You will need:

- two jacket potatoes
- two ice lollies
- two cool bags
- thermometer
- timer or clock

Work in groups and plan a test to see how a cool bag affects hot and cold food.

Think about:

- the best way to take the temperature of the foods
- how often to take the temperature of the foods
- what variables will need to be controlled
- why a potato and an ice-lolly should be left on the side as controls.

Draw and label a diagram of the test and control potatoes and ice lollies. Predict what you think will happen and why.

I predict that _____

because _____

_____

_____

Activity 3: Results table

Measure the temperature of the potatoes and lollies at the start before you put one of each in their separate cool bags. Then measure their temperature at the given number of minutes after the start. Use this table to record your temperature readings over this time for all four items.

| | Time (number of minutes after start) | | | | | | | | | |
	Start	1	2	5	10	15	20	25	30	Total temperature loss (°C)
Temperature (°C) of potato in a cool bag										
Temperature (°C) of ice lolly in a cool bag										
Temperature (°C) of potato not in a cool bag										
Temperature (°C) of an ice lolly not in a cool bag.										

Activity 4: Results bar graph

Use your results to create a bar graph.

The title of this graph is _____

The graph is to record _____

_____

_____

Look at the results. What do they show? What does this tell you about cool bags?

_____

_____

_____

_____

Key learning

In this lesson I have learnt: Some materials are **thermal insulators**. This means they conduct heat poorly. We use thermal insulators when we want to stop things from losing heat too quickly or warming up too quickly. Things like wool and feathers are natural thermal insulators. Other materials like polystyrene and fibreglass are synthetic. Some materials are **thermal conductors**, meaning they conduct heat very well. We use thermal conductors when we want things to heat up quickly, for example when cooking. Metal is used for saucepans because it is an excellent thermal conductor.

Homework

Safely observe and record examples of thermal insulators and conductors you can find outside of school.

Key vocabulary

absorb/absorbent   compost   contamination   decompose
environment   impermeable   permeable

Activity 1: Comparing reusable and disposable nappies

Some nappies are reusable, meaning you can wash them and use them again. Other nappies are disposable, meaning they are only used once.

Look at and carry out a series of comparative tests on a reusable nappy and a disposable nappy. Score each of the properties in this table, leaving one row empty for now.

You will need:
- reusable nappy
- disposable nappy

Type of nappy	Disposable	Reusable
Ease of use		
Comfort		
Flexible		
Elastic		
Absorbent		
Leak-proof		
Water-proof		
Overall score		

Explain your scoring system _____

_____

Which nappy would you choose and why? _____

_____

How could your tests have been improved? _____

_____

Activity 2: Environmental impact of nappies

Research the positive and negative points for using reusable and disposable nappies.

Disposable nappies		Reusable nappies	
Positive points	Negative points	Positive points	Negative points

Now go back to your first table. Add the heading 'eco-friendly' to the blank row. How does this change your overall scores?

_____

Which type of nappy do you think is best? Why?

_____

_____

_____

Key learning

In this lesson I have learnt that: Nappies need to be **absorbent** to help to keep babies clean. They have a **permeable** layer that absorbs liquid and an **impermeable** layer that stops any leaks. There are pros and cons to disposable and reusable nappies. Thousands of disposable nappies go to landfill every day. They never fully **decompose** and they can **contaminate** the **environment**. Reusable nappies do not cause plastic pollution, but it takes water and energy to wash them.

Homework

Look for any absorbent, permeable and waterproof materials at home. Think about why the items need the properties.

Earth and space

Lesson 1   What's in space?

Key vocabulary

diagram   light   light source   moons   solar system   star   planet

Activity 1: Space facts

Read these statements. Tick (✓) the boxes to say if you think the statements are true, false, or if you are not sure.

	True	False	Not sure
1. We see stars in the sky because they reflect the Sun's light.			
2. Stars have a shape with points.			
3. Stars give off light from burning gases.			
4. The Sun is a star.			
5. There are a lot of stars in our solar system.			
6. The Sun and Moon are the same size.			
7. There are many moons in the solar system.			
8. The Sun, Moon and Earth are circular.			
9. The Sun is not a star because it doesn't shine at night.			
10. There are no other solar systems in space.			
11. We see the Moon because it reflects the Sun's light.			
12. There are eight planets in our solar system.			
13. The Moon goes round the Sun.			
14. The Earth goes round the Sun.			
15. The Moon is a planet.			
16. The Sun moves behind the Moon at night.			
17. The Sun moves behind the Earth at night.			
18. The Earth stays still and everything moves around it.			

Activity 2: The solar system

Draw a labelled diagram of the solar system. Use the data in the table to help you see the order of the planets from the Sun, and to understand the size of each planet. Try to draw your diagram as accurately as possible.

Planet	Average distance from the Sun (million km)	Diameter (km)
Mercury	58	4,879
Venus	108	12,104
Earth	150	12,756
Mars	228	6,792
Jupiter	779	142,984
Saturn	1,434	120,536
Uranus	2,873	51,118
Neptune	4,495	49,528

Sun

Key learning

In this lesson I have learnt that: It's easier to see **stars** at night because the less **light** there is, the more visible the stars are. All stars are **light sources**. Our Sun is the star at the centre of our **solar system**. Other objects in the solar system include **planets** and **moons**. There are eight planets in our solar system. Each planet is a different size and a different distance from the Sun.

Homework

Learn the mnemonic My Very Educated Mother Just Served Us Noodles to help you remember the order of the planets. Try teaching it to someone at home, or even coming up with your own!

Key vocabulary

model   observe   orbit   pattern   planet   solar system   year

Activity 1: Movement of the planets

Look at this image of the solar system. Draw lines to show how you think each planet orbits the Sun.

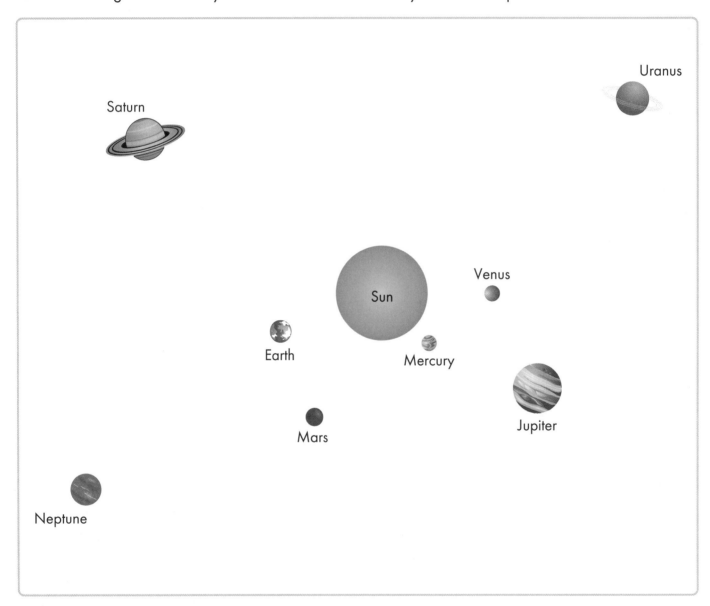

Circle the words to complete the sentences.

I predict that the planets closest to the Sun will have the slowest/fastest orbit.

I predict that the planets furthest away from the Sun will have the slowest/fastest orbit.

Activity 2: How do planets orbit the Sun?

The data in this table shows the length of one year on each planet, rounded to the nearest whole number. Use the information in this table and your findings from Activity 1 to answer the questions.

Planet	How long the planet takes to complete one orbit of the Sun
Mercury	88 Earth days (0.24 of an Earth year)
Venus	225 Earth days (0.6 of an Earth year)
Earth	365 Earth days (1 Earth year)
Mars	687 Earth days (1.9 Earth years)
Jupiter	12 Earth years
Saturn	29 Earth years
Uranus	84 Earth years
Neptune	164 Earth years

Look back at your predictions in Activity 1. Were they correct? Discuss with a partner.

What shape is the orbit of a planet?

_____

How long does the Earth take to orbit the Sun?

_____

What did you find out about the orbits of the planets that are closer to the Sun than the Earth is?

_____

_____

What did you find out about the orbits of the planets that are further from the Sun than the Earth is?

_____

_____

Key learning

In this lesson I have learnt: The **planets** in our **solar system** travel around the Sun. We call this path of movement their **orbit**. It takes Earth one **year** to orbit the Sun. The other planets have shorter or longer years depending on their distance from the Sun. All of the planets orbit the Sun in an anti-clockwise direction. Scientists have used **models** of the solar system to understand the **patterns** of the movement of the planets.

Homework

Research the terms 'heliocentric model' and 'geocentric model'. What do they mean? Can you explain them to someone at home?

Key vocabulary

diagram   light source   opaque   pattern   predict/prediction   shadow

Activity 1: Shadow enquiry

You will need
- a pencil
- a torch
- sticky tack

Work with a partner to tack a pencil vertically on a table and shine a torch on it. Observe what happens to the pencil's shadow in the different situations below, then complete the sentences.

When the torch is moved higher, the shadow _____

When the torch is moved lower, the shadow _____

When the torch is moved to the left, the shadow _____

When the torch is moved to the right, the shadow _____

Draw and label a diagram or a sequence of diagrams to show the outcomes of your enquiry below.

Activity 2: The position of the Sun

Use the words to label the diagram of where the Sun is at different times of the day.

afternoon	east	midday	morning	sunrise	sunset	west

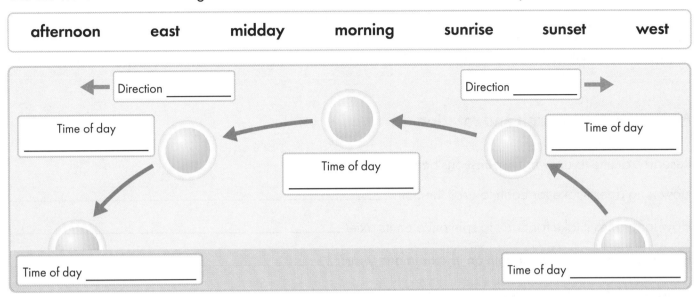

Direction _____

Time of day _____

Direction _____

Time of day _____

Time of day _____

Time of day _____

Time of day _____

Draw the shadow of the tree for each position of the Sun. Think about how it changes in size and position. Label your shadows 1 and 2.

Key learning

In this lesson I have learnt that: The Sun appears to move across the sky. We must never look directly at the Sun, but we can safely track its movement by looking at **shadows**. All **opaque** objects cast a shadow. The placement of the shadow depends on the position of the **light source**. By looking for **patterns** in shadows, we can make **predictions** about how they will change as the Sun moves across the sky.

Homework

With an adult, research how shadow clocks or sundials work and explain to your classmates.

Key vocabulary

explain/explanation   axis   dark/darkness   light   orbit   rotate   Sun

Activity 1: Earth's orbit and rotation

Research online to answer the questions below.

How long does it take for Earth to orbit the Sun? _____

How long does it take for Earth to spin once on its axis? _____

How many times does Earth spin on its axis in one year? _____

Activity 2: Day and night

Find where you live on the globe and stick the small figure there. Shine the torch or lamp on the opposite side of the globe. Use your model to demonstrate what causes day and night. Write a commentary below to accompany your demonstration, using the words in the box.

You will need
- a globe
- a torch or lamp
- a small paper figure

24 hours	day	midday	sky	afternoon	daytime
morning	Sun	appears to move		Earth	night
sunrise	axis	evening	rotate/rotation		sunset

_____

_____

_____

Key learning

In this lesson I have learnt that: As Earth **orbits** the **Sun**, it **rotates** on its **axis**. When parts of the Earth face the Sun and receive **light**, it is daytime. When parts of the Earth face away from the Sun, it is **dark**, and that is night time. It takes 24 hours for Earth to rotate once on its axis.

Homework

Choose a country far from where you live. Find out what time it is there now.

Key vocabulary

axis   evidence   model   moon   orbit   planet   rotate   solar system

Activity 1: Moon phases

The Moon is not a light source. We can only see it because it reflects light from the Sun. It takes about 28 days for the Moon to rotate on its axis, and to orbit Earth. During that time, it looks like the Moon changes shape.

Can you explain why this is evidence that the Moon is not a light source?

_____

_____

_____

_____

Why is the Moon not a planet?

_____

_____

How long does it take for the Moon to rotate on its axis?

_____

Activity 2: Models of the solar system

For thousands of years, scientists have observed the skies and come up with different **models** of the solar system. They used their observations as **evidence** to support their models. Over time, equipment has become more powerful and allowed us to see more objects in space. New models were created using the new evidence.

Research different models of the solar system and label the models with the time periods to show how our understanding of the solar system has changed.

| 300 BCE | 200 CE | 1620s | 1850s |

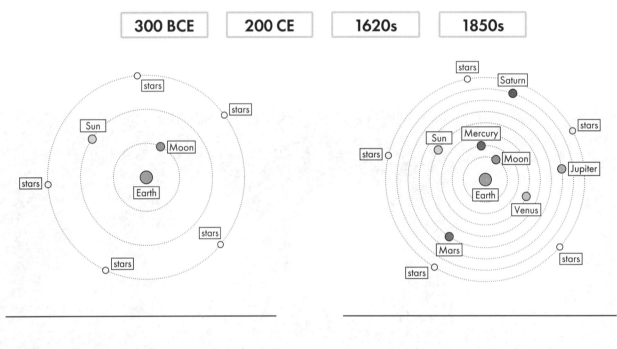

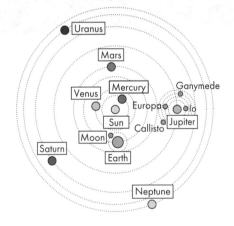

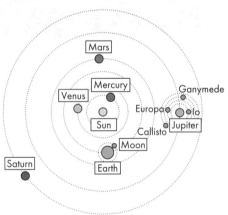

If you found out the meaning of 'heliocentric' and 'geocentric', include this information on the diagrams.

Activity 3: How the Moon moves

Draw an annotated diagram to show how the Moon moves around the Earth. Think about its orbit and how it rotates on its axis.

Tick (✓) the statements that are scientific evidence that support your diagram.

The Moon appears to change shape during each month. ☐

The Moon is a sphere of rock. ☐

We usually see the Moon at night. ☐

We always see the same moon craters and mountains facing the Earth. ☐

Key learning

In this lesson I have learnt that: The Sun is the centre of our **solar system**, and eight **planets orbit** around it. There are other bodies in the solar system as well, like **moons** and dwarf planets. Earth has a **moon** – simply called the Moon! It is not a planet because it does not orbit the Sun. Instead, the Moon orbits Earth. The Moon also **rotates** on its **axis**.

Homework

Find out about recent advances in space exploration and observation, for example the Hubble Telescope and James Webb Space Telescope (JWST), the Perseverance Mission to Mars, the International Space Station, or Voyager 2.

Key vocabulary

data   model   orbit   pattern   planet   predict/prediction   solar system

Activity 1: Do planets further from the Sun have longer years?

Look at the information on the table and at the scatter graph that uses the data. Answer the question below and explain your answer.

Planet	Average distance from the Sun (million km)	Length of a year (Earth years)
Mercury	58	0.24
Venus	108	0.6
Earth	150	1
Mars	228	1.9
Jupiter	779	12
Saturn	1,434	29
Uranus	2,873	84
Neptune	4,495	164

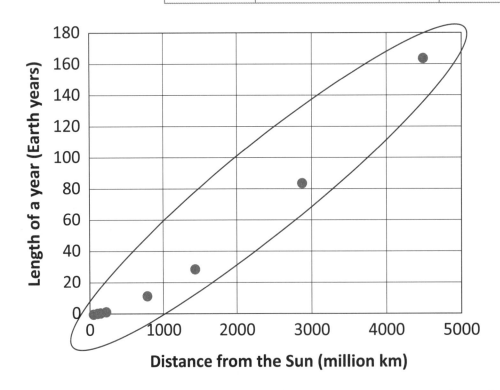

Do the planets further from the Sun have longer years? Explain your answer using evidence from the graph.

_____

_____

Activity 2: Do larger planets have more moons?

Use the graph to answer the question and state if there is a pattern or not.

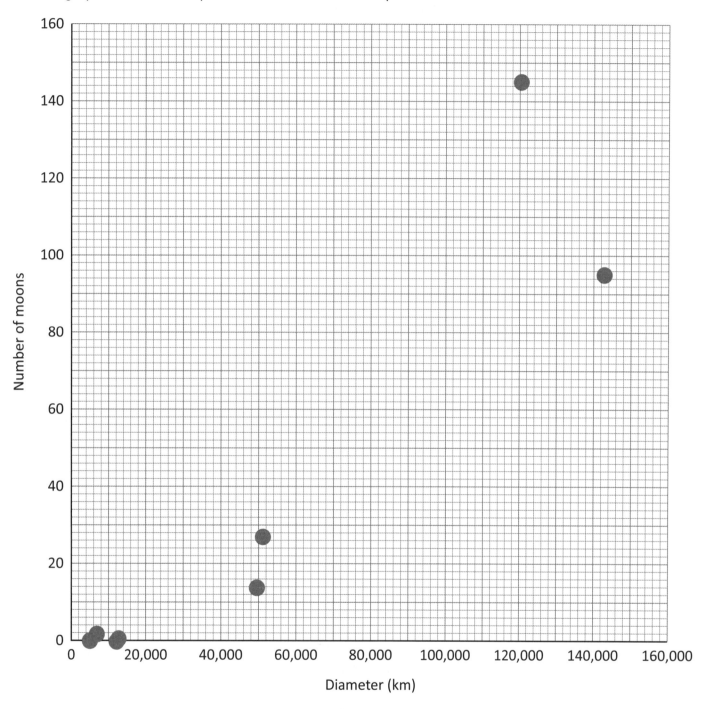

Do larger planets have more moons? Explain your answer using evidence from the graph.

_____

_____

_____

Activity 3: Do larger planets have longer years?

Use the graph to answer the question and state if there is a pattern or not.

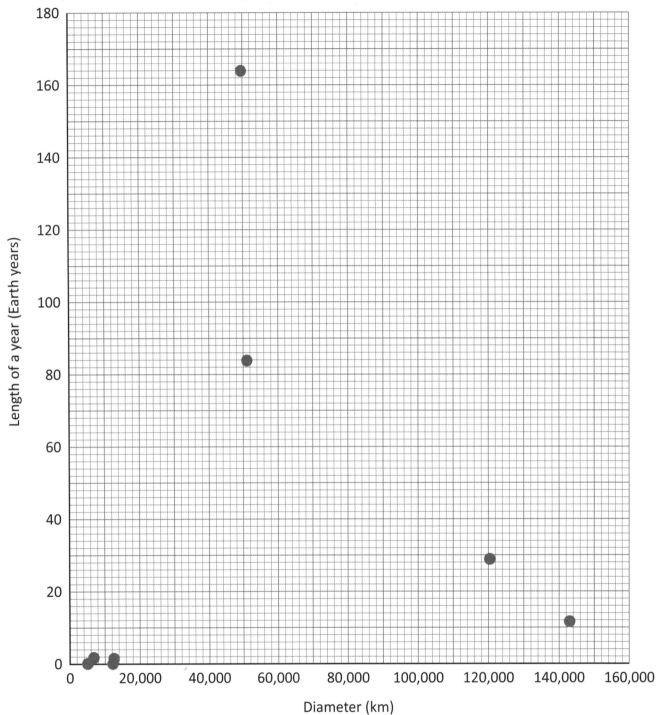

Do larger planets have longer years? Explain your answer using the graph.

_____

_____

_____

Activity 4: Do planets that are further from the Sun move more quickly?

Use the graph to answer the question and state if there is a pattern or not.

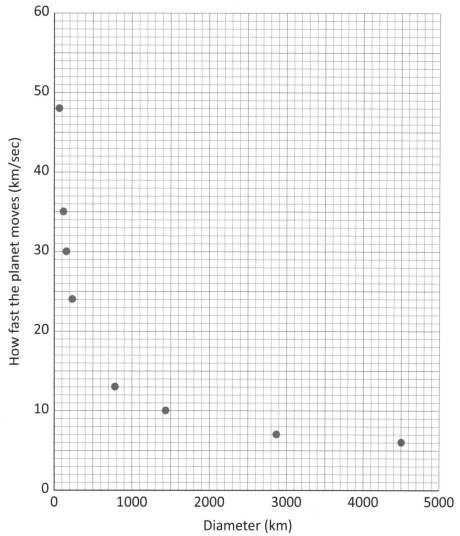

Do planets that are further from the Sun move more quickly? Explain your answer using the graph.

_____

_____

Key learning

In this lesson I have learnt: By creating **models** and collecting **data**, we can identify **patterns**. These patterns – or lack of a pattern – can support or refute our **predictions**. Scientists have learned a lot about our **solar system** and how the **planets orbit** the Sun by creating models and using their observations.

Homework

Explain to someone at home your three favourite new things that you have learned during this module.

Plant and animal life cycles

Lesson 1 How do flowering plants produce seeds?

Key vocabulary

anther   carpel   filamen   ovary   ovule   pollen   stamen   stigma   style

Activity 1: Life cycle of a flower

Write a number 1–4 under each picture to show the order of the life cycle of a flower. Next to the number, write the correct label below to describe each stage:

fertilisation   flowering   pollination   seed formation

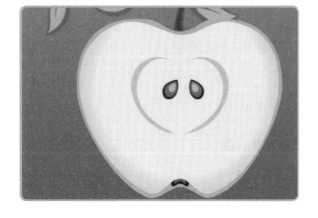

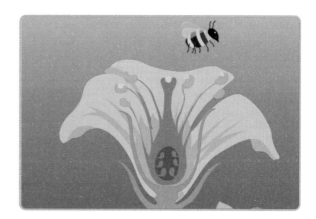

_____

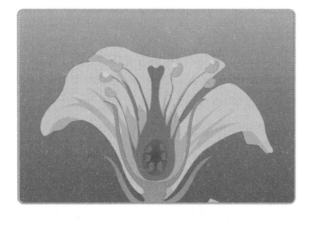

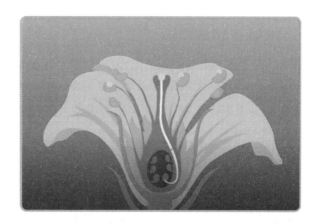

_____

Activity 2: Flower dissection

Look at a flower carefully. Draw and label a picture of it in the box below. Include labels for petals, stamens, carpels, stigma, style, ovary, sepals.

Complete the sentence.

Pollinators would be attracted to this flower by _____

_____

_____

Dissect your plant. Observe it closely using a magnifier.
Draw a labelled diagram of the stamen.

Draw a labelled diagram of the carpel.

Activity 3: Flower parts

Use what you've learned so far to label the parts of the flower on this diagram.

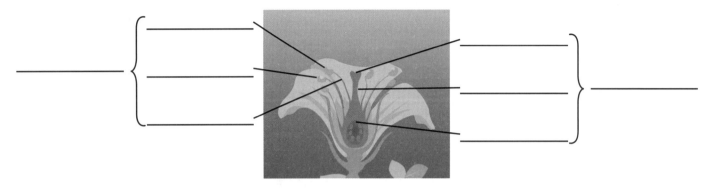

Activity 4: True or false?

Tick (✓) a box next to each statement to show if it is true, false or not always true.

What would happen if there were no bees or insects to pollinate the plants?

	True	False	Not always true
The carpel is the female part of the flower, where the seed is made.			
The stamens are the male part of the flower. They produce pollen.			
Flowers are only pollinated by insects.			
Some plants don't have colourful flowers.			
Seeds are always found inside fruit.			
Only some flowers produce nectar.			

Key learning

In this lesson I have learnt that: Flowers need **stamens** and **carpels** to reproduce. The stamen is the male part of the flower, and contains the **filament** and the **anther**. **Pollen** is made in the anther. The carpel is the female part of the flower, and contains the **stigma**, the **style** and the **ovary**. Pollen fertilises the **ovule** inside the ovary, and seeds are produced.

Homework

Have a look for seeds where you live. Collect and draw some of the seeds you find.

Key vocabulary

anther   carpel   filament   ovary   ovule   pollen   stamen   stigma   style

Activity 1: Parts of a flower

Draw lines to match each flower part with the correct definition.

carpel	male part of a flower made up of a filament and an anther
stigma	the female reproductive cell of plants
stamen	the part of the carpel that contains the ovules or eggs
anther	female part of a flowering plant which contains an ovary, style and stigma
filament	part that is made by flowers and from which a new plant can grow
pollen	the stalk of a stamen
ovary	part of the carpel, leads from the stigma to the ovary
ovule	fine yellow powder made by the anthers of flowering plants to help them make new plants
seed	the end part of a stamen, containing sacs where pollen matures
style	the top of the carpel which takes in pollen

Activity 2: Comparing flowers

Look carefully at two different flowers. Compare them with each other. Use a magnifier to help you to look closely, then fill in the table below.

	Flower one	Flower two
Draw the flowers.		
How many petals does it have?		
How many stamens does it have?		
Draw the shape of the stigma.		

Activity 3: Flower tally chart

Go on a flower hunt. Record the colour and number of stamens for each flower you find in the tally chart.

Number of stamens	White	Yellow	Orange	Red	Pink	Purple	Blue	Green
1–5								
More than 5								

Draw two flowers that you find.

Complete the information.

Shape: _____   Shape: _____

Number of stamens: _____   Number of stamens: _____

Did you notice any pattern between the number of stamens and the colour or shape of the flower?

_____

_____

Key learning

In this lesson I have learnt that: Different flowers have different numbers of petals, **stamens** or **carpels**, and that this helps botanists to identify them.

Homework

Find a plant outside school or near your home. Look at it for a few minutes and write a list of describing words or phrases about your plant. Draw the leaf and any other important features, such as flower, fruit, pine cone, catkin, bark. Or why not try writing a poem about your plant?

Key vocabulary

asexual   propagation   reproduction

Activity 1: Plant propagation

Watch the Snap Science video online on Plant propagation or do your own research. Complete the sentences about propagation using the words in the box.

bulbs	tubers	cuttings	clone	parent	runners	asexual	split

When a plant creates a new plant by itself, we call it _____ reproduction. The new

plant is a _____ , meaning it is identical to its _____ .

Some plants, like daffodils, grow from _____ . Other plants, like potatoes, grow from

_____ . Some plants grow long _____ , like strawberry

plants. Gardeners can take _____ from plants to grow new ones, and some plants

can be _____ at the roots.

daffodil bulb

potato tuber

Activity 2: Growing plants without seeds

Read the instructions for propagating plants on the next page. Choose one plant. Use the correct instructions to propagate a new plant.

> Can you think of some reasons why gardeners like to propagate their favourite plants?

You will need
- plants that can be propagated in the three different ways described, for example lavender, rosemary, strawberries, spider plants, geraniums
- scissors
- plant pots
- compost
- rooting powder
- lolly sticks

Propagating from softwood cuttings, for example lavender or rosemary:

- Use scissors to cut a piece of a stem about 10 cm long, just above the leaf on a parent plant.
- Remove the leaves from the bottom half of the cutting.
- Take off half the leaves that are left.
- Dip the bottom end into the rooting powder.
- Insert the cutting into a pot of moist compost, keeping the lower leaves just above compost level.
- Cover the pot loosely with a transparent plastic bag held in place with an elastic band or string.

Propagating from runners, for example strawberries or spider plants:

- Cut a runner off from the parent.
- Transplant the plantlet into a pot.

Propagating by dividing, for example geranium:

- Small, fibrous-rooted plants can be lifted and pulled apart gently.
- Plant the small clumps in compost in small pots.

Complete the sentences then answer the question.

The plant I am growing: _____

How I propagated it: _____

How is propagating plants different to growing them from seeds? _____

_____

Leave your plant to grow for a few weeks. Draw your plant.

Key learning

In this lesson I have learnt that: When pollen moves from the male reproductive part of a plant into the female reproductive part of the same type of plant, seeds are produced. This is called sexual **reproduction**. Some plants can reproduce without pollen. We call this **asexual** reproduction. The plant can **propagate** without needing two parent plants.

Homework

See if you can find any plants growing in cracks or small spaces around where you live. Find out their names. Explain how you think they got there, and if this was because of sexual or asexual reproduction.

Key vocabulary

embryo   hatch   mate   vertebrate

Activity 1: Inside an egg

Label the diagram of the egg using the words from the box. One has been done for you.

shell   membrane   air cell   albumen   chalaza   yolk   germinal disc

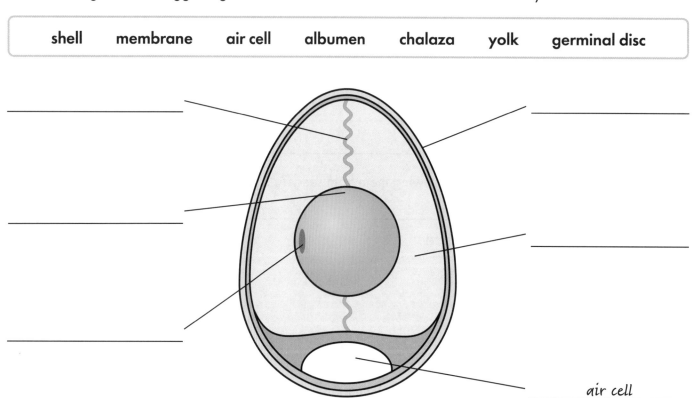

_____

_____

_____

air cell

What do you already know about birds? Tick (✓) true or false for each statement.

	True	False
All birds can fly.		
All birds build nests.		
Birds' nests are always made from sticks.		
All birds lay eggs.		
Some birds nest underground.		

Find out about the life cycle of a chicken. Draw pictures and make notes about each stage.

Key learning

In this lesson I have learnt that: Animals that have a backbone inside their body are called **vertebrates**. Birds are one of the five vertebrate groups. Most animals **mate**, meaning they reproduce sexually. Birds lay eggs, and if the egg has been fertilised, the **embryo** will grow into a chick and **hatch**.

Homework

Get birdwatching! Sit in a quiet place, by a window or outside. Watch and see how many birds you can spot in ten minutes. Draw a picture of a bird that you spotted. Where was it? How big was it? What was it doing?

Key vocabulary

embryo   fertilisation   mammal   gestation   life cycle   reproduction

Activity 1: Mammals fact sheet

Find out about the mammals in the table below. Answer the questions and complete the table.

You will need
- books and online resources about mammals

	Pipistrelle bat	African elephant	Mountain gorilla	Polar bear
Describe the observable features of the animal.				
What does it eat?				
Where does it live?				
How long does it live?				
How many young does it have each year?				
What do the young look like when they are born?				

Activity 2: Gestation periods in mammals

Do you think the mammals on page 60 all have the same gestation period? Research each mammal to complete the table.

Animal	Gestation period (days)	Average female adult weight (kg)
Pipistrelle bat		0.008
Grey squirrel	44	0.06
Miniature Schnauzer dog	62	7
Suffolk sheep	147	88
Mountain gorilla		98
Polar bear		250
Jersey cow	278	400
African elephant		3,000

Activity 3: Gestation periods in mammals bar chart

Use the table from Activity 2 to create a bar chart. Put the animals in order of weight, starting with the lightest. Use the prompts and the headings in the table to write the axis labels on your graph.

Look at your bar chart. Answer the questions.

Can you see a pattern between the adult's weight and the gestation period?

_____

_____

Are there any animals in the bar chart that don't follow this pattern?

_____

Activity 4: Life cycles of birds and mammals

Compare the life cycle of birds and mammals. Answer 'yes' or 'no' to each question.

	Mammals	Birds
Does sperm from the male fertilise eggs inside the female?		
Do eggs develop into embryos inside the female?		
Do eggs develop outside the female?		
Do the young feed on milk from their mother?		

Find out about kangaroos and duck-billed platypuses. How are their life cycles different to the mammals you have already looked at?

Key learning

In this lesson I have learnt that: Animals are divided into invertebrates and vertebrates. **Mammals** are one type of vertebrate. When they have reached the adult stage of the **life cycle**, they can **reproduce**. If an egg is **fertilised**, the **embryo** grows in the mother's womb. Once the baby is fully grown, it is born. The time it takes for a baby to fully develop in the womb is called the **gestation** period.

Homework

Create a fact file about an endangered mammal. Why is it under threat? What can be done to save it?

Lesson 6 — How do amphibians change throughout their life cycle?

Key vocabulary

amphibian   bird   fertilisation   life cycle   metamorphosis

Activity 1: Common frog life cycle

Research the life cycle of the common frog. Draw pictures and label each stage. Use the words in the box.

You will need
- books and online resources about the common frog

| egg | spawn | tadpole | froglet | frog | mate | fertilise |

Activity 2: Comparing tadpoles and frogs

The common frog goes through metamorphosis, which means it goes through lots of different changes to become an adult. Compare the differences between a tadpole and a frog by completing the chart.

	Tadpole	Frog
How is the life cycle of a common frog similar to the life cycle of a chicken? How is it different?		
What does it look like? • **How many back legs?** • **How many front legs?** • **Does it have a tail?** • **Where are its eyes?**		
What does it eat?		
Does it live in the water, on land or both?		
How does it breathe?		

Key learning

In this lesson I have learnt that: **Amphibians** can live on land and in water. Like **birds**, they lay eggs. However, their eggs are soft and are laid in water. A male and a female mate to **fertilise** the eggs. Amphibians can lay hundreds or even thousands of eggs at a time! Amphibians go through extreme changes as they move through their **life cycle**. This is called **metamorphosis**.

Homework

Find out about toads and axolotls. Write a list of the differences between adult toads and adult axolotls.

Key vocabulary

exoskeleton   insect   larva   metamorphosis   pupa   life cycle   thorax

Activity 1: Young and old

Caterpillars are butterfly larvae. Butterflies are the adults. Caterpillars undergo metamorphosis to become butterflies. Look at the photos and write a list of differences between the caterpillar and the butterfly.

caterpillar

butterfly

Differences between a caterpillar and a butterfly:

- _____
- _____
- _____
- _____

Stick insects undergo an incomplete metamorphosis. Look at the photos and write a list of how the stick insect nymph (young) and the adult are different.

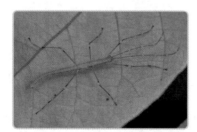
stick insect nymph

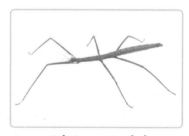
stick insect adult

Differences between a stick insect nymph and a stick insect adult:

- _____
- _____
- _____
- _____

Activity 2: Comparing insect life cycles

You will need
- books and online resources about insects

Find out about the differences between butterflies and stick insects. Use the table to note your answers.

	butterfly	stick insect
What are their eggs like?		
How long do the eggs take to hatch?		
What comes out of the egg?		
Do they have a pupa stage?		
Do the adults look like the young?		
Do they go through complete or incomplete metamorphosis?		

Key learning

In this lesson I have learnt that: **Insects** are invertebrates. They have a hard covering, called an **exoskeleton**. Their bodies are made up of the head, the **thorax** and the abdomen. The **life cycle** is different for different insects. Some go through a complete **metamorphosis**, which has four stages: egg, **larva**, **pupa**, adult. The adult insect looks completely different from the lava. Other insects go through an incomplete metamorphosis, which only has three stages. The adult insect looks very similar to the young insect.

Homework

Look carefully around the school or your home for evidence of insects. Make a note of what you find and where. Take photos or draw pictures of what you see.

Separating mixtures and changing materials

Lesson 1   How can we separate mixtures?

Key vocabulary

explain/explanation   mixture   separate   sieve   solid

Activity 1: Separating mixtures

Look at the mixture of solids in the mixtures below. Do you think each mixture could be separated? How could you do it? Complete the sentences.

The two solids in this mixture are _____

They could be separated by _____

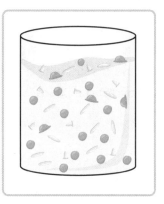

The two solids in this mixture are _____

They could be separated by _____

Activity 2: Sorting mixtures

Create eight sets of mixtures of two different materials, such as dried peas and paperclips, or sugar and toy spiders. Swap your mixtures with other students in your class. Work with a partner to separate the mixtures you have been given using different equipment, such as sieves made from paper plates, magnets, spoons and other items.

Use this grid to name the solids that you find. Write what equipment you tried out, and if you were able to successfully separate the solids from each other.

	Solids identified	Equipment used	Was the separation successful?
1			
2			
3			
4			
5			
6			
7			
8			

Key learning

In this lesson I have learnt that: We can group materials by their state of matter – that's whether they are a **solid**, a liquid or a gas. When we combine a solid with a solid, or a solid with a liquid, we call it a **mixture**. Sometimes, we might need to **separate** a mixture. We do this in different ways depending on the materials that make up the mixture.

Homework

See if you can find any equipment at home that works in a similar way to a **sieve**. For example, a slotted spoon or a colander. Draw and label a diagram of the item and explain how it would be helpful for separating different mixtures.

Key vocabulary

dissolve   evaporate / evaporation   insoluble
saturated   soluble   solution

Activity 1: Soluble and insoluble

Look at the photos below showing sand and salt in glasses of water.

Which of these solids is soluble? _____

Which of these solids is insoluble? _____

Underneath each picture, explain how you might separate the solid from the liquid.

sand and water

_____

_____

_____

salt and water

_____

_____

_____

Activity 2: Dissolving solids

Place a solid in the beaker and add water. Observe the solid sitting in the water, then stir the solid and water together. Observe what happens to the solid. Repeat with the other solids in turn each in a fresh beaker.

Record your findings in the table on the next page.

You will need

- a selection of solids, such as sugar, salt, sand, flour, tea leaves, powder paint, coffee granules
- water
- beakers
- measuring jugs
- spoons

Name of solid	My observations		Did the solid dissolve or not?
	after adding water	after stirring	

Answer the questions.

Which solids dissolved? _____

What happened to the solids when they dissolved? _____

What happened to the solids that did not dissolve? _____

Choose one solid. Answer the questions.

Describe what you noticed when you added the water to the solid. _____

_____

Describe any changes you saw straight away. _____

_____

Did stirring your solid help? _____

_____

Key learning

In this lesson I have learnt that: When two solids are combined, they make a mixture. We can also combine solids and liquids. Some solids are **soluble**, which means they **dissolve** in liquid. Some solids are **insoluble**, which means they do not dissolve in liquid. When a soluble solid and liquid mix together, we call it a **solution**. When no more solid can be dissolved into a liquid, the solution is said to be **saturated**. If the liquid **evaporates**, the solid will be left behind.

Homework

Observe different activities at home, like washing up, preparing meals and cleaning. List any examples you find of solids dissolving in liquids.

Key vocabulary

comparative test   dissolve   reversible   saturated   solution

Activity 1: Dissolving solids

Read the statements. Tick (✓) the boxes to show if you think they are true, false or you are not sure.

	True	False	Not sure
If you can't dissolve any more solid, the liquid is saturated.			
Some powders dissolve a bit and what's left stays in the water.			
Dissolved coloured sugar is dissolved even though you can still see its colour.			
Some solids can dissolve in liquids other than water.			
Some types of sugar take much longer to dissolve than others.			
You can't get back a dissolved solid.			
Some solids don't dissolve, but they don't form a suspension (float through the liquid) either.			
Sugar dissolves more quickly when the water is hot.			
When water is cold you can't dissolve anything.			

Can you think of any ideas for ways to make a solid dissolve faster? Discuss your ideas with a partner.

Activity 2: Comparative test: dissolving rate

Carry out a comparative test to find out what makes the most difference to the time it takes for a solid to dissolve in water. Choose a variable to test, for example: stirring, amount of solid, the shape and size of the solid, the volume of water and the temperature of the water. Choose the solid you are testing, then write your prediction and plan a method for your test.

You will need

- different types of salt or different types of sugar
- transparent beakers
- spoons
- a timer
- a thermometer
- water of different temperatures

Prediction

I am going to test what might affect the rate at which _____ dissolves.

The variable I am going to change is _____

The variables I am going to keep the same are _____

Explain how you think changing the variable will affect the rate at which the solid dissolves.

_____

_____

Method

I am going to test my prediction by _____

_____

_____

_____

_____

Create your own table to record your results.

Activity 3: Reflect and review

Use the different test results from your class to answer the following questions.

Which variable seems to have made the solid dissolve fastest? _____

Which variable do you think had the least effect and why? _____

_____

Activity 4: Is this change reversible?

The word 'reversible' describes a material change where the materials involved can change back to their original state.

Once a solution has been made by dissolving sugar or salt in water, do you think it is possible to reverse the change? Explain your answer.

_____

_____

Pour a small amount of dissolved salt or sugar solution from your investigation into shallow containers or saucers. Leave the containers in different places around the classroom and observe and record any changes that happen before the next lesson.

> **What difference would the amount of solution in the saucer make to the time it takes for the solid to reappear? Discuss with a partner.**

> **What do you think has happened? Discuss with a partner.**

> **What else could you change to affect how quickly the solid reappears? Discuss with a partner.**

Key learning

In this lesson I have learnt that: If a solid is soluble, it will **dissolve** in liquid. This mixture is called a **solution**. If there is too much of the solid, the liquid will eventually become **saturated**. No more solid will dissolve. If the solid and liquid can be separated again, we call this a **reversible** change.

Homework

If someone in your family puts sugar in their tea or coffee, explain to them why they should stir their tea or coffee before drinking it.

Key vocabulary

contamination	crystal	dissolve	evaporate
filter	reversible	solution	

Activity 1: Separating mixtures

Complete the sentences about separating mixtures. Use the words in the box to help you.

dissolve	evaporate	reversed	solution	crystals	filters	contaminated

A _____ is made when a solid _____ in a liquid. Sometimes, this change can be _____ . For example, if we leave a solution of salt and water out, eventually the water will _____ and salt _____ will remain.

We can also use sieves and _____ to separate solids and liquids. These are particularly good when cleaning _____ water.

Activity 2: Filtering water

Mix together water with a range of different sized solids in a bucket. Next, design a filter bed that will clean the particles out of your water.

You will need

- water mixed with soil, sand, pebbles, leaves, twigs and bits of plastic
- a bucket
- large selection of rocks, pebbles, gravel, course sand, fine sand
- wadding, felt or other thick fabric, filter paper
- large plant pots, or buckets with holes

Answer the questions below.

How will your filter bed remove the largest particles from the water?

_____

How will your filter bed remove the smallest particles from the water?

_____

How many times will you need to filter the water?

_____

Use this table to plan how you will create and then use your filter bed to filter the water to make it as clean as possible.

	Process
Step 1	
Step 2	
Step 3	
Step 4	
Step 5	
Step 6	

Answer the questions below.

Did your filter bed completely clean your water? Explain your answer.

_____

How could you remove any further solids from the water?

_____

Activity 3: Reflect and review

Use your filter bed to filter your bucket of dirty water.

Draw a side-on, cut-away view diagram of your filter bed. Annotate your diagram to explain how each part of the filter cleaned the water.

Key learning

In this lesson I have learnt that: When a solid **dissolves** in a liquid, it creates a **solution**. Sometimes, the liquid can **evaporate** and the solid will be left behind. This is an example of a **reversible** change because the solid and the liquid are no longer mixed together. Sometimes, water can be **contaminated** by solids that dissolve in it. We can use **filters** to help separate out the solids from the water.

Homework

Find out about different water filters. Look at water filtering jugs or swimming pool filters. Are there any other ways to filter water?

Key vocabulary

carbon dioxide   gas   liquid   non-reversible   reversible   solid

Activity 1: Reversible and non-reversible changes

Complete the table to consider reversible and non-reversible changes.

	Reversible or non-reversible?	How do you know?
boiling water		
melting ice cream		
cooked food		
sugar in tea		

Activity 2: Which mixture produces the most gas?

Carry out a comparative test to find out which mixture of a liquid and a solid (for example vinegar and bicarbonate of soda) produces the most gas.

Plan which mixtures you are going to test. Create a table with three columns. Write your mixtures in the left hand column. Carry out your tests and record your results in the second column and your observations in the third column.

You will need

- beakers • teaspoons
- water, white vinegar and lemon juice • bicarbonate of soda, tartaric acid, baking powder and vitamin C tablets
- plastic bottles • elastic bands • disposable gloves • a timer

Which mixture creates the most gas? Place a fresh version of your mixture in a bottle and put a disposable glove over the mouth of the bottle. Seal the bottle with elastic bands. Time how long it takes for the glove to inflate. Repeat with different proportions of solid and liquid and time again.

Summarise the results of this final test.

_____

_____

_____

Key learning

In this lesson I have learnt that: Many chemical changes, such as mixing baking soda with vinegar, are **non-reversible**. In this instance, a **gas** called **carbon dioxide** is produced, which cannot be changed back to the **solid** and **liquid**.

Homework

Write a list of reversible and non-reversible changes you can identify at home.

Key vocabulary

carbon dioxide   non-reversible   reversible

Activity 1: Non-reversible changes

You will need

- a soluble vitamin C tablet
- water

Predict what you think will happen if you add small pieces of a vitamin C tablet to water.

Complete the sentence.

I predict that _____

_____

Carry out the enquiry, adding pieces of vitamin C tablet to the water one at a time. Write one or two sentences about what happened. Use some of the words in this box for your explanation.

gas	liquid	rapidly	reversible	solid	water
slowly	produce	tablet	after	non-reversible	
will	change	always	dissolve	with	bubbles

Do you know what gas is released when you mix a vitamin C tablet with water?

_____

_____

_____

Activity 2: Planning a fair test

You will need

- small containers with lids
- a plastic tray
- soluble vitamin C tablets
- water
- sticky tack
- a tape measure

Carry out this activity with an adult to keep you safe.

Create your own rocket. Put a small amount of water in the bottom of a container and stick a blob of sticky tack inside the lid. Push the tablet into the sticky tack and put the lid on the container. Quickly turn the container over and place it in a plastic tray.

Decide how you will measure how high the container flies, for example mark on the wall at the point where the rocket starts to fall.

Plan how you will carry out a fair test to see if changing the amount of water or tablet will change how high the rocket will fly.

Be careful not to return to your 'rocket' before it has taken off.

The variable we are going to change is: _____

The variables that must stay the same are: _____

I predict that _____

My method for this fair test will be:

_____

_____

_____

_____

Activity 3: Results and conclusion

Carry out your fair test. Record your results in a table that you have designed below. Decide how many columns you need and what headings you will use.

Circle the correct answer then complete the sentence. My prediction was correct / incorrect because

_____

Key learning

In this lesson I learnt that: If you can mix two or more things together then separate them out again, that is a **reversible** change. If it is impossible to put things back to how they were, that is a **non-reversible** change. One example of a non-reversible change is mixing vinegar with bicarbonate of soda to create **carbon dioxide**.

Homework

With an adult at home, find a video online that shows the diet cola and sweets experiment. Explain to an adult what is happening and why, and what type of change is taking place.

Human growth and reproduction

Lesson 1   How do newborn babies change into teenagers?

Key vocabulary

gestation   infancy   life cycle   mammal

pregnancy   reproduction   umbilical cord   uterus

Activity 1: How have I changed?

Talk to a partner about how you have changed since you were a newborn baby. Answer the questions below.

What can you do now that you couldn't do when you were a baby?

_____

What can you do now that you couldn't do when you first started school?

_____

Activity 2: Gestation

Humans have a life cycle. It happens in three stages. The first stage begins when the child is growing inside its mother. This is called the gestation stage of the life cycle. When a baby is growing inside a mother's body, we say that the mother is pregnant.

Read the information below about the gestation period and answer the questions.

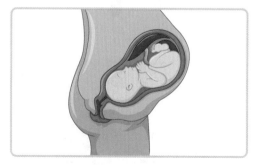

The baby grows in the uterus, in the abdomen of the woman's body.

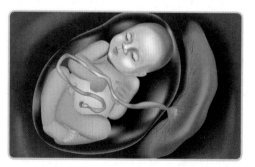

The baby is attached to the mother's bloodstream by the umbilical cord, so it doesn't need to breathe or eat for itself. The food eaten by the mother and the oxygen breathed in by the mother reach the baby in the blood.

Answer the questions.

What is the first stage of the human life cycle called?

_____

Where does the baby grow?

_____

What attaches the baby to the mother's bloodstream before it is born?

_____

Activity 3: Infancy

Babies and toddlers are at the stage of the life cycle called infancy. Infancy lasts for around two years.

What can a baby do? What can a two-year-old child do? How independent are they at this age? Think about any infants you know. Talk about your ideas with a partner. Use this space to make notes.

_____

_____

_____

_____

_____

Activity 4: Childhood

What can a child do that an infant can't? What have you learned to do since you were five years old? Talk about your ideas and the research you've done with a partner. Use this space to make notes.

_____

_____

_____

_____

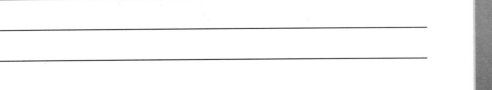

Activity 5: Human development milestones

Use the chart below to note down how humans change from babies to teenagers. Think about changes in the body, physical abilities, self care and independence, learning, social skills and so on.

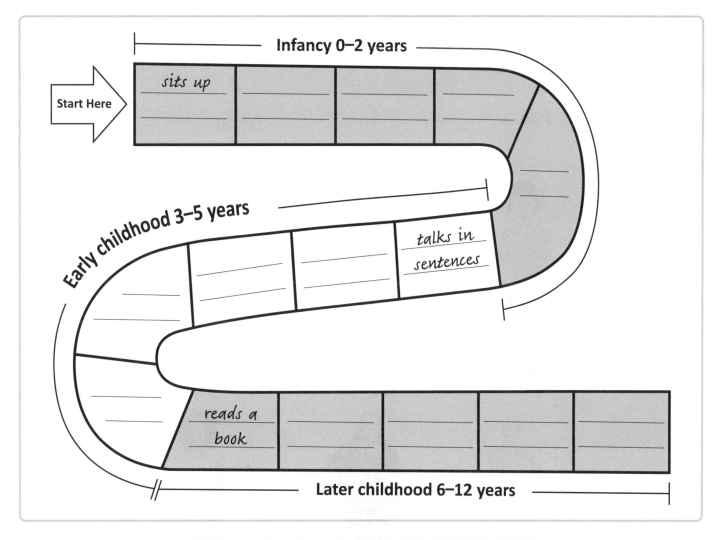

Infancy 0–2 years

Start Here

sits up

Early childhood 3–5 years

talks in sentences

reads a book

Later childhood 6–12 years

Key vocabulary

girl   woman   teenager

Activity 1: Girls and women

Look at each picture and decide if it is a woman or a girl. Talk to a partner about how you know and write notes below.

_____

_____

_____

_____

_____

_____

Activity 2: Girl to woman

Use your research about what happens when a girl changes to a woman to create a poster with the title 'Things all girls need to know by the age of 10'.

Do all girls change in exactly the same way and at exactly the same time? Talk to a partner and then discuss as a class.

Key learning

In this lesson I have learned that: Humans change from newborns to teenagers. **Teenagers** then change into adults. This stage of the human life cycle is called puberty. Boys and **girls** change in different ways.

Homework

Find out what the term 'period poverty' means. How does this affect girls and women? What can be done about it?

Key vocabulary

Adam's apple   boy   man   muscles   teenager

Activity 1: Boys and men

Look at each picture and decide if it is a man or a boy. Talk to a partner about how you know and write notes below.

_____

_____

_____

_____

_____

Activity 2: Boy to man

Use your research about what happens when a boy changes to a man to create a poster with the title 'Things all boys need to know by the age of 10'.

> Do all boys change in exactly the same way and at exactly the same time? Talk to a partner and then discuss as a class.

Key learning

In this lesson I have learned that: The time in our lives when we change from children to adults is called puberty. **Teenagers** then change into adults. **Boys** and girls change in different ways, for example boys develop larger **muscles** and their **Adam's apple** becomes more noticeable.

Homework

Think about a common myth about puberty, for example spots appear when someone is unclean or only boys get sweaty. Explain why your myth is not true and give evidence to support your answer.

Key vocabulary

adulthood   childhood   gestation   infancy   life cycle   pregnancy

Activity 1: Order the ages

Write numbers 1–8 below the pictures to put them in order, showing youngest to oldest.

_____   _____   _____   _____

_____   _____   _____   _____

Complete the sentences using different photographs each time.

I think _____ is older than _____ because I can see that _____ .

I think _____ is older than _____ because I can see that _____ .

I think _____ is older than _____ because I can see that _____ .

I think _____ is older than _____ because I can see that _____ .

Activity 2: The phases of human life

Draw lines to link each picture with the correct life stage.

old age

infancy

birth

teenager

pregnancy

adulthood

childhood

Activity 3: Adulthood and old age

Complete the sentences about adulthood, ageing and death. Use the words in the box to help you.

hair	skin	death	adulthood	reproduce	exercise
	ageing	life cycle	active	body	strongest

The stage after puberty is _____ . Most adult humans can _____ , and it is

during this stage that humans are at their _____ . Our bodies start to change because of

the _____ process. Signs of ageing include _____ turning grey,

_____ becoming wrinkled and the _____ gets weaker. However, things

like _____ , socialising and keeping an _____ mind can help people to live

well and happily through their old age. Eventually, the body stops working. This is when _____

occurs. It is a natural part of the _____ and happens to all living things.

Activity 4: The human life cycle

Which of these would be the best diagram to use to show the human life cycle? Circle 1, 2 or 3. Then use the space below to draw your life cycle diagram. Use the words in the box to complete your diagram.

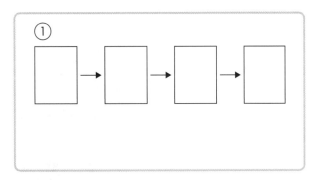 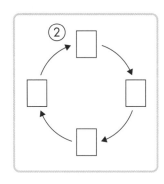 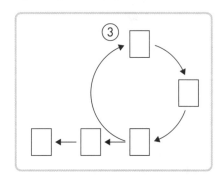

| teenage | adulthood | birth | childhood | old age | death | gestation | infancy |

Activity 5: Using evidence to determine age

Use evidence from the images to work out how old each person is. Record your evidence in the table.

I think this person is ____ ____ old	I think this person is ____ ____ old	I think this person is ____ ____ old	I think this person is ____ ____ old
Evidence:	Evidence:	Evidence:	Evidence:

Key learning

In this lesson I have learnt that: Humans are mammals and have their own **life cycle**. The life cycle starts with birth and ends in death. After the **gestation/pregnancy** stage, a child develops through **infancy** into **childhood** and finally into **adulthood**. A human changes throughout adulthood as they get older. For example their skin becomes wrinkled, their hair grey and their body weakens.

Homework

Look at some other photographs of humans – either people you know or in magazines. How old do you think they are? At which stage of the human life cycle are they at? Look for evidence to support your ideas.

William Collins' dream of knowledge for all began with the publication of his first book in 1819.
A self-educated mill worker, he not only enriched millions of lives, but also founded a flourishing publishing house. Today, staying true to this spirit, Collins books are packed with inspiration, innovation and practical expertise.
They place you at the centre of a world of possibility and give you exactly what you need to explore it.

Published by Collins
An imprint of HarperCollins*Publishers*
The News Building, 1 London Bridge Street, London, SE1 9GF, UK

HarperCollins*Publishers*
Macken House, 39/40 Mayor Street Upper, Dublin 1, D01 C9W8, Ireland

Browse the complete Collins catalogue at
collins.co.uk

10 9 8 7 6 5 4 3 2 1

ISBN 978-0-00-868326-9

British Library Cataloguing-in-Publication Data
A catalogue record for this publication is available from the British Library.

Development Editor: Kathryn Kendall Boucher
Series Editor: Jane Turner
Consultant Reviewer: David Allen
Publisher: Laura White
Copyeditor: Kariss Holgarth
Proofreader: Sarah Snashall
Cover Designer: Amparo at Kneath Associates
Packager: Oriel Square
Typesetter: Tech-Set
Production Controller: Alhady Ali
Printed and bound in Great Britain by Martins the Printers

This book contains FSC™ certified paper and other controlled
sources to ensure responsible forest management.

For more information visit: www.harpercollins.co.uk/green

collins.co.uk/sustainability

Acknowledgements
This work is adapted from the original work, Snap Science Second Edition Year 5
All images are from Shutterstock.

The publishers gratefully acknowledge the permission granted to reproduce the copyright material in this book. Every effort has been made to trace copyright holders and to obtain their permission for the use of copyright material. The publishers will gladly receive any information enabling them to rectify any error or omission at the first opportunity.